W9-CCB-892

Coco

COCO
CHANEL

For

Gwyneth Hume,

my Grandmother.

Just like Coco, you were a woman of class,
strength and gusto!

COCO
CHANEL

THE ILLUSTRATED WORLD OF A FASHION ICON

Megan Hess

hardie grant books

Contents

—

Introduction

Few people in the history of fashion can claim the influence of Coco Chanel. From her humble beginnings to the many heartaches she faced throughout her life, her story is one of strength, determination and creative vision.

As a fashion illustrator, I have been endlessly fascinated and inspired by the little French orphan girl who single-handedly reshaped women's wardrobes, and created the fashion staples we still wear today.

What separated Coco Chanel from other designers was her originality and her sheer will to never steer away from the vision that she so strongly believed in. She designed, lived and loved with gusto. She refused to take 'no' for an answer and she forged ahead with self-belief, regardless of the obstacles in her way.

Looking at images of Coco Chanel, I wonder what she might have thought in her later years when she reflected back on her life – from her early childhood of struggle, to the excitement and drama that she first created in her tiny atelier, to the success of the House of Chanel that she built. I imagine she would have been very proud indeed. I wonder if she ever really understood how many people, such as myself, she has truly inspired.

When Chanel shows in Grand Palais in Paris each season, I like to picture Coco watching from above from her famous mirrored staircase, overseeing her classic designs recreated many times over on a world stage.

This book is the illustrated story of Chanel's life - an insight into her magical world, the iconic designs she created, and the empire of the House of Chanel.

01

the Woman

The life of Gabrielle 'Coco' Chanel is shrouded in mystery. Perhaps because she was uncomfortable with her humble beginnings, Chanel had a reputation for obscuring her past – glossing over details, dismissing transgressions and painful memories. Just as she reinvented fashion, cutting and re-cutting a sleeve forty times over, she did the same to her past. Though there are few accounts of her youth, it is clear that Chanel had a difficult start to life: raised in poverty after losing her mother and being abandoned by her father. Without the support of parents at a young age, she endured a lonely childhood in an orphanage in Aubazine in rural France.

Perhaps it was the difficulties of her early life that inspired her to pursue a radically different path, first as a performer, then as a milliner, and eventually the iconic fashion designer she became. Chanel would rise above her circumstances to forever revolutionise fashion for women in the modern era. Her beauty and flair won her many friends and admirers; the most celebrated figures of the century – Cocteau, Diaghilev, Picasso, Dalí, Stravinsky and Churchill – sought her company. The creative vision of her designs would live on as trademarks of an iconic fashion brand.

Chanel was born in 1883 in Saumur, a market town on the river Loire.
The illegitimate daughter of a laundrywoman and a merchant, Chanel was twelve when
her mother died and her father left her in a convent in the town of Aubazine.

It was here in the orphanage that Chanel
learned the art of survival.

Though most young girls of the
era were taught how to sew,
Chanel had a natural flair for
needlework and honed her skills
during school vacations spent
with her grandparents in the
provincial capital of Moulins.

These holidays were a pleasure that offered respite from life at the orphanage.

Bored and miserable at the convent, Chanel absorbed the austere beauty of her surroundings. Her strict uniform, featuring a white blouse and black pleated skirt would later influence her trademark silhouette.

The beige, black and white of the nuns' habits, their rosary beads, crosses and chains would also emerge as emblems throughout her career.

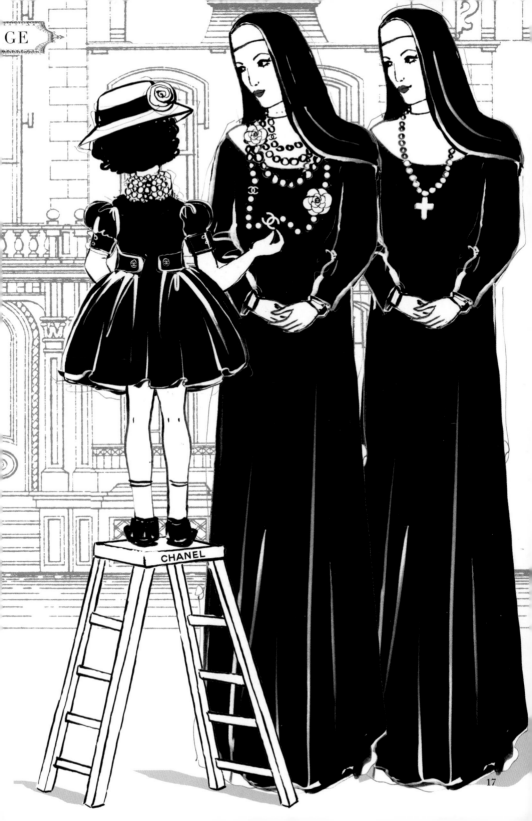

CHANEL

Chanel left the convent in Aubazine for the Notre Dame school in Moulins, where her aunt Adrienne, only a year her senior, was being educated. Chanel's sartorial abilities caught the attention of the Mother Superior, who found employment for her and Adrienne as shop assistants in a local draper's store on the Rue de l'Horloge.

The girls shared an attic bedroom above the shop, working on weekends for a nearby tailor where they altered breeches for cavalry officers stationed in the town.

Chanel and Adrienne
socialised with the local
gentlemen, many of
whom were in the army
and would often take
them out dancing.

"

in order
TO BE IRREPLACABLE
one must
ALWAYS BE
different

"

When not plying her trade with a needle, Chanel dreamed of becoming a singer. Her stage debut came at La Rotonde, a popular entertaining pavilion in the park of Moulins, where she accepted a regular spot performing with a local cabaret.

Here she sang with Adrienne on an evening slot, later going on to perform solo.

Chanel won over the crowds with her youth and charm, and eventually moved to Vichy, her first adventure, to establish a singing career.

Chanel created many stories of how she earned
her sweet moniker 'Coco'. She was baptised
Gabrielle Chanel after a nun in the hospice where she
was born. *'My father used to call me "Little Coco" until
something better should come along,'* she once
told journalist Marcel Haedrich in an interview.
A more likely story, however, is that she acquired it
during her days as a performer.

The crowds at La Rotonde would
call out 'Coco' to her, referring to
the two popular songs Chanel
would sing: 'Qui qu'a vu Coco',
about a Parisian girl who
had lost her dog, and 'Ko Ko
Ri Ko', a French version of
'Cock-a-doodle-doo'.

COCO CHANEL

Throughout her career, Chanel often dismissed the name Coco – and yet she was proud of its recognition. The fact that it became so well known remains a testament to her indisputable influence.

Around age twenty, while Chanel
was at Vichy, she met Etienne Balsan,
an ex-cavalry officer and textile heir. Chanel
ran away with Balsan and the two became lovers,
leaving behind the girl, Gabrielle, to become Coco.

During her years with Balsan, Chanel resided as his cocotte at his estate in Royallieu in Compiègne where Balsan kept a racing stable. It was at Royallieu with Balsan that Chanel had her entry into high society. Balsan is often depicted as the wealthy playboy who introduced Chanel, a poor seamstress, to a life of baroque pleasures and excess – yet Chanel also took full advantage of Balsan for his powerful connections, using his status to help set up her business. Later, it was in the ground floor of Balsan's Paris apartment that Chanel began her millinery label. Despite his infidelities, Balsan displayed a lifelong loyalty to Chanel. The two continued to be friends until his death in 1953.

Chanel was first noticed for her millinery
skills, a medium in which she was quick to
carve out her own style.

Under her millinery label, she produced boater
hats stripped of the embellishments, frills and
furbelows that were fashionable at the time.

She dismissed such ornament as unnecessary
and cumbersome, weighing a woman down.

'Nothing makes a woman look older than obvious
expensiveness, ornateness, complication,'
she said to writer Claude Delay in old age,
still wearing her original, modern designs,
'I still dress as I always did, like a schoolgirl.'

" it is

ALWAYS

better to be

SLIGHTLY

underdressed

"

Chanel's millinery designs were revolutionary for the time, reflecting her personal style. In her dress, she would borrow elements from menswear that emphasised comfort over decorative constraint. It was at the racing stables of Royallieu that Chanel first began to wear jodhpurs, shirtsleeves and unadorned felt hats, pioneering the functional versatility of sportswear.

For riding, women would customarily pair their jackets and white shirts with long, heavy skirts – never pants. Chanel had jodhpurs tailored to her figure and stood out in the sea of corsets, laces, flounces and frills.

Even when wearing more conventional womenswear, Chanel opted for a longer, looser fit. The effect was the coquettish, *gamine* silhouette that has come to define her style.

At Royallieu, Chanel became smitten
with one of Balsan's friends, a wealthy,
handsome upper class Englishman.

His name was Arthur Capel,
but was known endearingly
by his friends as 'Boy'.

BOY CAPEL

Though there were rumours around Capel's origins, many of them swathed in romance, what is known is that he was a wealthy businessman from a prosperous English family. Like Balsan, Capel was an accomplished polo player and notorious playboy. Capel – who is often depicted as Chanel's great love – showed much faith in Chanel, loaning her the sum to start her millinery business.

COCO CHANEL

Capel was a businessman who understood finances and appreciated Chanel's talent and ambition. Though Capel was forever in the company of other women and would go on to marry Diana Wyndham, he continued his affair with Chanel until his sudden death in 1919.

With the support of Balsan, Chanel opened a
millinery boutique in Paris in 1908 in the ground
floor of his apartment at 160 Boulevard Malesherbes.

Chanel adored her time in Paris,
and with her business flourishing
she quickly attracted a loyal following.

With her clientele swiftly expanding,
she soon had a staff of three and sought new premises.

45

"

MY LIFE DIDN'T
please me

SO I CREATED
my life

Nestled beside the fashionable Place Vendôme and Rue du Faubourg Saint-Honoré, Chanel Modes was in the heart of Paris and the centre of Paris haute couture.

Word spread and she became a favourite of Parisian socialites, including the leading actresses of the day, Lucienne Roger and Gabrielle Dorziat, who modelled her hats in Fernand Nozière's play *Bel-Ami* in 1912.

Chanel Modes helped to establish Chanel's reputation. Her designs – simple, elegant and chic – caused a sensation and were imitated across the city.

Chanel would often model the hats herself and by 1912 they were regularly featured in the leading fashion press, such as the periodical *Les Modes*.

Business was booming and Chanel soon achieved financial independence. The terms of her lease at 21 Rue Cambon, however, prevented her from selling clothes, as there was another dressmaker working in the building.

An obstacle, like many others in her life, Chanel quickly overcame.

Chanel is often associated with the glamour
of Paris, but a greater influence for the
designer was the northern seaside town of
Deauville, where she spent many happy
vacations with Capel. Deauville is largely
cited as the birthplace of Chanel's
clothing career. It was here she was
inspired by what she saw on the
tennis court, at the races and in
the harbour.

After seeing the French sailors' uniforms,
the designer incorporated nautical elements
into a chic sensibility for the modern woman,
decreeing that pea jackets, striped pullovers
and bell-bottomed pants were *de rigueur*.

Inspired by the cosmopolitan lustre of Deauville, Chanel seized the opportunity to open her maison de couture in 1913, producing high-end designs for the leisure class that holidayed there.

Experimenting with comfortable beachwear and sportswear, it was here that Chanel began to use jersey, a material that draped well and complemented the natural form of the body. The decision was at first a practical one; postwar shortages meant short supply of more expensive fabrics, and jersey was one of few options she could afford in bulk. Chanel tailored the fabric to her simple and practical designs including her one-piece swimming costumes that came halfway down the thigh, a length scandalous for the time.

As Chanel said, *'I make fashions women can live in, breathe in, feel comfortable in.'* Success in Deauville encouraged Chanel to expand her business to Biarritz, on the Basque coast, in 1915.

CHANEL

Chanel embodied the practical simplicity
of her clothes and the modern woman.
She drew from the sensibility of menswear,
a look she coupled with her irresistibly
chic, chin-length bob.

The Coco Bob

As Chanel told Claude Delay, the hairstyle came about by accident. The story goes that she was going to the opera with her thick hair done up in braids, but her gas burner exploded, covering her in soot.

Undaunted, Chanel took a pair of scissors and slashed her braids. As she said, *'A woman who cuts her hair is about to change her life.'*

" luxury must BE COMFORTABLE, otherwise IT IS NOT luxury "

down the street from her existing premises. The space became the backbone of

CHANEL

CH

Looking to expand her business in Paris, Chanel bought the entire building at 31 Rue Cambon in 1918,

the House of Chanel and an iconic
architectural symbol for the brand.

CHANEL

It was an emporium of Chanel: selling
clothes, hats and accessories, make-up and
beauty products, and eventually jewellery
and fragrance as well.

The interior of 31 Rue Cambon is dominated by a famous mirrored staircase that leads from the ground floor entrance to the haute couture salon on the first floor,

and then upward to
Mademoiselle's private
apartment and design studio.
However, with no bed in the
apartment the designer slept at the
Hotel Ritz across the road, where
she maintained a lavish studio
as a private suite.

Each morning, Chanel would cross Rue Cambon from the Hotel Ritz to the House of Chanel, telephoning first so her attendants could spritz the salon with Chanel N°5 for her arrival.

The designer maintained a high standard of detail at the House of Chanel;
she would have the scent sprayed in the dressing rooms of the salesroom before
opening the doors to clients. The scent lingers there today, drifting around the
mirrored staircase to her private apartment upstairs.

A wealth of personal touches can be found in
Chanel's upstairs apartment at 31 Rue Cambon.

The space, once used to entertain Salvador Dalí,
Elizabeth Taylor and Pablo Picasso, remains a
bird's nest of eclectic objects and furniture collected
by the designer.

Throughout her life Chanel amassed a unique
collection of treasures: a painting, *The Ear of Wheat*,
by her friend Salvador Dalí, an ancient Russian icon
from Igor Stravinsky, a bronze sculpted hand by the
artist Diego Giacometti and golden boxes given to
her by the Duke of Westminster.

Coco Chanel's favorite café was Angelina and she reportedly would go there daily, just for the hot chocolate. She always sat at table number 10, which was positioned next to one of the mirrors. Chanel loved mirrors and used them to coyly keep an eye on the world around her.

Embraced by a glamorous following of Paris elite, the House of Chanel thrived. Chanel managed the workroom to high standard, overseeing the rigid structure of her haute couture salon lead by the *premières d'atelier*, who were responsible for the production of the designs for her haute couture clients.

The garments were then tailored and hand-finished by the *petite mains*, the women whose task it was to sew the designs.

BOY CAPEL
22.12.1919

On 22 December 1919, Boy Capel died suddenly in a motorcycle accident, apparently while on his way to see Chanel.

Chanel was devastated by the loss; as well as being a financial support, Capel deeply influenced Chanel's career and style.

While mourning Capel's death, her friends, artist José Maria Sert and his wife Misia, convinced her to accompany them to Venice.

At the time, Venice was a major transit point for trade between the East and West, and it was here that Chanel discovered the Orient. Her new surroundings instilled in her a taste for opulent colours, breaking away from her usual palette of black and white. The city was home to Byzantine gold and sculptures of lions – the emblem of the city. The lion was also the emblem of Chanel's zodiac sign, Leo, and she adopted this as the symbol for the house. Venice would become a continual source of design inspiration.

"

in
LOSING
Capel
I LOST
everything

HE SHAPED ME,
he knew how
TO DEVELOP WHAT WAS
unique in me,
AT THE COST OF
everything else
"

02

the Brand

Coco Chanel never produced a ready-to-wear collection and yet she revolutionised the concept, forever changing the way women dress. Chanel's designs were inspired and brave: she was one of the first to design women's trousers, brought black from mourning dress to eveningwear and introduced the use of jersey from the realm of sportswear to luxury dress. Chanel's comfortable and elegant aesthetic would resonate through the decades.

The first half of the twentieth century was a time that saw a dramatic shift in the role of the sexes. Chanel's *gamine* silhouette and shortened hemlines, now synonymous with the brand, allowed women to discard their corsets and embrace modernism. Chanel was a woman who designed for other women, delivering garments that mirrored their changing role in society.

Her signature details – tweed fabrics, monochrome colour palette, gold chains, quilted leather and the interlocking 'C' logo – endure to this day. A pioneering force, there is no denying her genius and impact on the fashion world.

How did the world's most iconic fragrance come about?
Released in 1921, the formula was developed by perfumer
Ernest Beaux, who ran a laboratory in Grasse.

Beaux created a range of samples for the designer
and Chanel chose his fifth concoction, naming it so
after her lucky number.

AMPLES

N° 6
CHANEL
PARIS
PARFUM

N° 11
CHANEL
PARIS
PARFUM

N° 12
CHANEL
PARIS
PARFUM

At the time perfumes were typically replicas of floral scents, however N°5 reflected a new approach because it was an abstraction of over eighty perfume essences.

Chanel spoke of N°5 as
'a woman's perfume, with a woman's scent.'
The amber-coloured liquid contains the essence
of jasmine, ylang-ylang and May roses combined
with synthetic aldehydes, apparently added by mistake.

The fragrance was a roaring success, and, amid
steady sales, Marilyn Monroe helped turn it
into a twentieth-century obsession.
When she was asked during an
interview for *Time* magazine
what she wore to bed, she
responded *'just a few drops
of Chanel N°5.'*

The iconic Chanel N°5 glass bottle, designed by Chanel, debuted the interlocking 'C' logo on its seal. Simple and elegant, the square-faceted bottle is decidedly Art Deco.

The octagonal stopper, cut like a diamond, recalls the geometry and proportions of Place Vendôme, the Parisian square home to the Hotel Ritz.

In 1959, New York's Museum of Modern Art honoured Chanel by exhibiting a bottle of N°5 in its collection.

The two interlocking 'C's that form the Chanel logo are instantly recognisable. Yet – much like the couturier's life – there are several stories about how the design came about.

Besides being the designer's initials, the interlocking
design is reminiscent of the stained-glass windows in the
Cistercian abbey in Aubazine where Chanel grew up.

The two 'C's might also suggest 'Chanel and Capel',
named after the love of her life. The monogram, which
was first created in 1921 for Chanel Nº5, has since become
synonymous with the brand.

The two 'C's motif would emerge repeatedly,
including on the buttons of Chanel clothing
and on the wax seal of the Nº5 bottle.

"

fashion
IS NOT
something
THAT EXISTS IN
dresses
ONLY

fashion
HAS TO DO WITH
ideas,
THE WAY WE
live
"

Throughout her oeuvre,
Chanel has focused
on a simple palette
of black, white, beige,
gold and red.

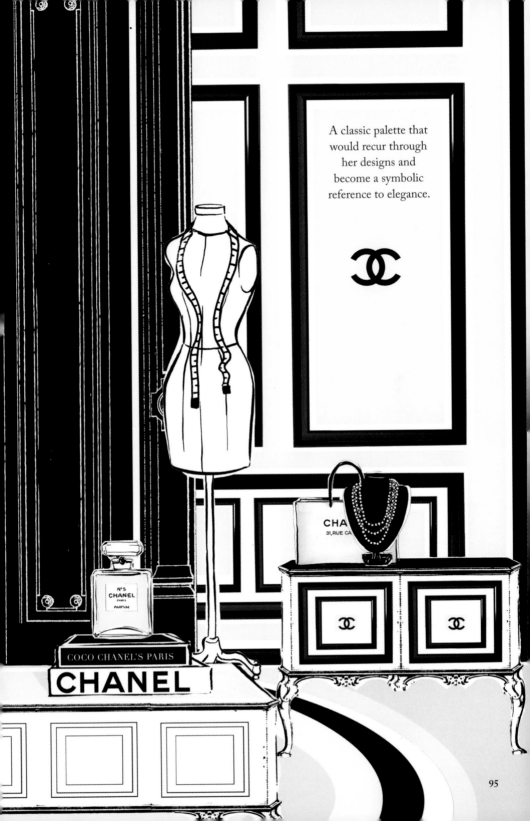

A classic palette that
would recur through
her designs and
become a symbolic
reference to elegance.

Red features in flashes, emerging in the details of her garments, such as the lining of her accessories.

Chanel also adored gold, using it in her costume jewellery and the chain-link straps of her coveted bags. But it is Chanel's use of black and white, perhaps inspired by the uniforms of the nuns of her childhood, that has come to define the house. Once seen as the colour of mourning, Chanel reshaped black to represent elegance.

The designer once famously said, *'I have said that black has it all. White too. Their beauty is absolute. It is the perfect harmony.'* While her well-to-do American customers made a point never to wear white post-Labor Day, Chanel transformed it into a year-round staple.

Chanel had the vision to turn black
into a symbol of independence,
freedom and strength for women.

A story goes that Chanel's rival designer
Paul Poiret stopped her on the street
in Paris, gazing disdainfully at her
shockingly simple black frock, asked,
'Who are you in mourning for, mademoiselle?'

The designer replied, *'For you, monsieur.'*

In 1926, illustrations of Chanel's design for
the black dress appeared in American *Vogue*.
The design featured a round neckline, long
sleeves and a skirt that sat just below the knees.

It was dubbed the 'Ford' dress, after the era's
democratic black Model T automobile. Just like
the car, the Little Black Dress was simple and
accessible for women of every class. The simple,
unstructured design in unlined *crêpe de chine*,
accented by four diagonal stripes, was decidedly
unfussy and would one day be, according to *Vogue*,
'*the gown that all the world will wear.*'

Today it is considered a classic, a pioneering
example of Chanel's radical simplicity.

"

fashion is
ARCHITECTURE
it is a
MATTER OF
proportions

"

One of the most iconic symbols of the House of Chanel is the tweed suit. It was released in the 1950s with a design that featured a collarless jacket with braided trim, fitted sleeves, metallic buttons and an accompanying skirt. The haute couture garment still features the same key

The classic cream Chanel Suit

functional details that mark its authenticity, such as the string of chain sewn into the jacket lining to weight the hem. A practical and chic style statement, it was a perfect choice for postwar women who were seeking to build a career in the male-dominated workplace of the time.

The Classic Chanel Cape

The classic

Chanel's use of tweed wasn't just inspired by menswear, but by one man in particular. That man was the Duke of Westminster, who Chanel met in 1923 and courted for seven years.

Chanel would borrow British sportswear from her beau and make his tweeds her own by sourcing fabric from a tweed mill in Scotland.

The trend spread when actress Ina Claire appeared in American *Vogue* in a brown tweed Chanel dress. It was dubbed 'Chanel's English Look' by the magazine.

Chanel would work with tweed fabrics from lightweight wools to weightier bouclés, transforming it into a luxury material.

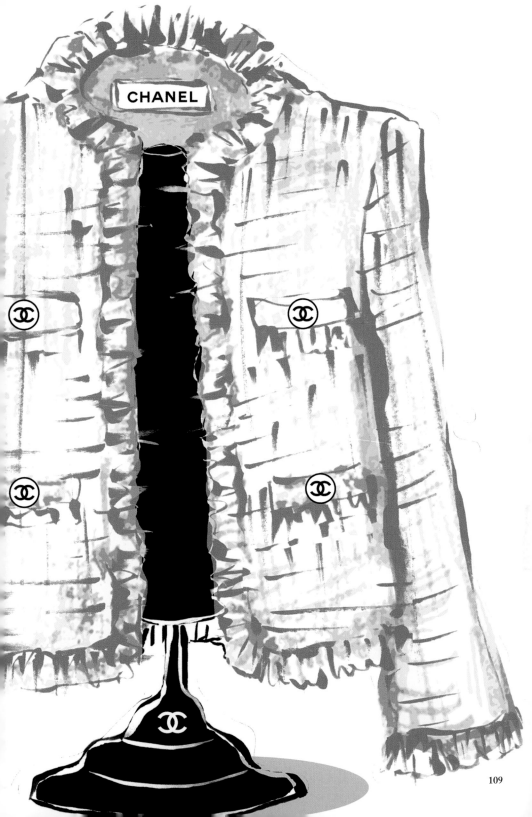

Another enduring symbol of the House of Chanel is the camellia. Some say the designer's love of the oriental bloom was inspired by memories of when elegant young dandies wore them pinned to the lapels of their jackets.

The Camellia

Or perhaps it was a reference to Alexandre Dumas's novel, *La Dame aux Camélias* (*The Lady of the Camellias*),

a story she was influenced by in her youth.

Enamoured by the flower, Chanel began to feature camellias throughout her designs from the early 1920s, pinning the silk flowers to her lapels and accessories. She would also feature the flowers on her purses and costume jewellery. To this day, the circular bloom remains a trademark of the brand.

Chanel's use of costume jewellery reflected her mantra that a woman should accessorise every outfit. She designed strings of pearls, semi-precious stones and gilded chains to be worn with casual daywear.

Chanel

Costume Jewellery

Chanel's costume jewellery, most of which was made by haute couture supplier Maison Gripoix, offered a more affordable means of ornamentation.

Inspired by Byzantine and
Renaissance iconography,
her jewellery pieces would
set expensive jewels into
a malleable plastic,
providing the
perfect foil for
her understated
clothing.

"

fashion fades

ONLY

style

REMAINS

the same

"

A key motif for the House of Chanel, pearls defined the designer's personal style. Chanel believed that the function of jewellery was not to flaunt one's wealth, but to be worn as ornamentation.

Chanel Pearls

In 1926, the designer created the fashion for mismatched earrings by wearing a black pearl in one ear and white in the other. Later, in 1954, Chanel collaborated with Robert Goossens to create her iconic costume jewellery.

Chanel was rarely seen without a pile of pearls around her neck and a pair of fabric scissors that hung from them, ready to tailor a garment at any moment.

Chanel began producing cosmetics in the 1920s, collaborating with the beauty manufacturer Bourjois to create beauty products as well as perfume for the house.

Being the most accessible
Chanel product, the
partnership would lay the
foundations of the beauty
empire that the brand
has become.

Chanel believed in the power of lipstick to seduce men and cure sadness. The designer created her first range of lipsticks in 1924 with the debut colour her favourite shade of classic red.

CHA
BE

The formula of intense red was released in an ivory flacon, embellished with black metal edges, in typical Chanel classicism. Today, one can still buy many different shades of red, Mademoiselle's favourite colour for lipstick.

" "

THE
Best colour
IN THE WHOLE
world
IS THE ONE THAT
looks good
ON YOU

" "

As well as making glamorous haute couture, Chanel also diversified into designing theatrical costumes.

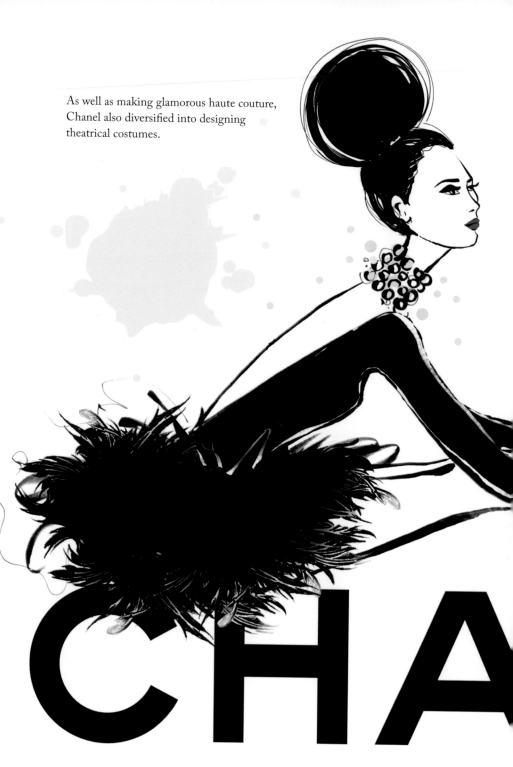

In 1922, she created Grecian-style dresses in coarse wool for Jean Cocteau's ballet adaptation of Sophocles' *Antigone*, with Pablo Picasso in charge of the set designs. The costumes were such a hit they featured in French *Vogue* that year and Chanel went on to design the stage costumes for Cocteau's *Orphée* in 1926. Cocteau explained his choice of Chanel, *'because she is the greatest couturière of our time. And I cannot imagine the daughters of Oedipus badly dressed.'*

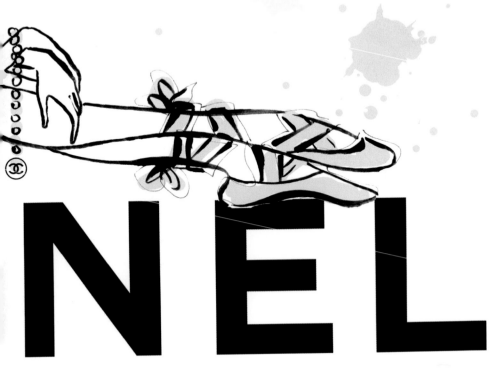

NEL

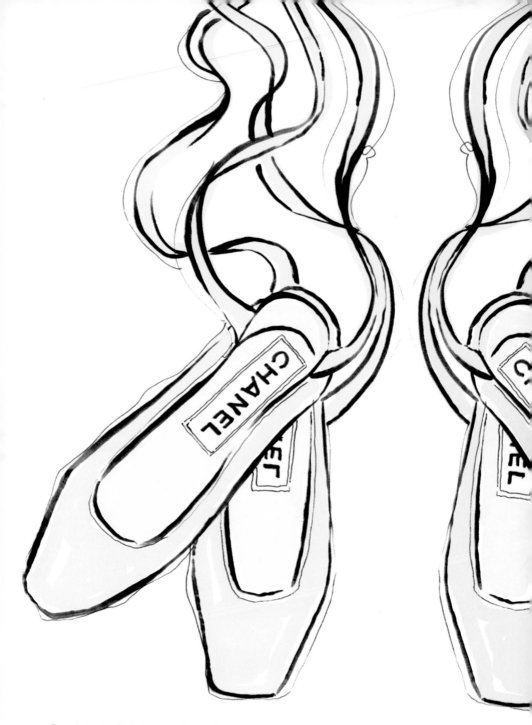

Socialising in Paris' artistic circles, Chanel became acquainted with Ballet Russes impresario Sergei Diaghilev, a collaborator who would become a lifelong friend.

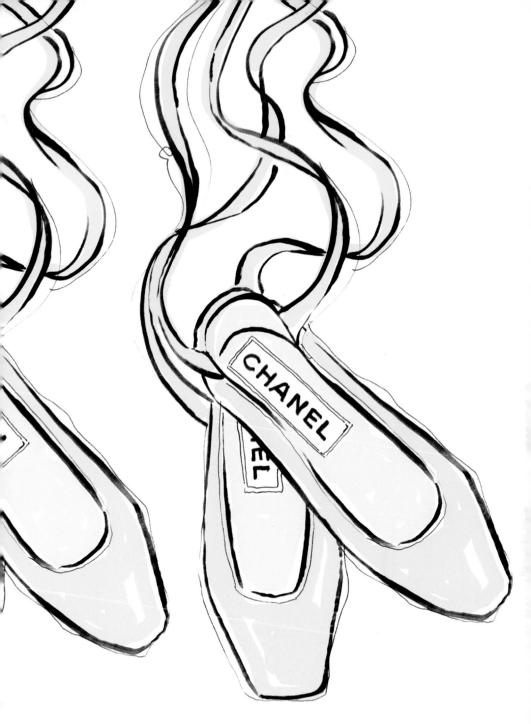

The designer created the provocative jersey swimsuits for the influential Ballet Russes in their modern-realist production of *Le Train Bleu* in 1924.

With her mounting fame as a designer, Chanel caught the attention of Hollywood moviemaker Samuel Goldwyn. In 1931 Goldwyn hired Chanel to design two annual collections for the leading Hollywood stars of the silver screen. Chanel would fly to Hollywood twice a year to create designs for his film studio Metro-Goldwyn-Mayer.

It was during this time – the years of the Great Depression – that Chanel created looks for the films *Palmy Days*, *The Greeks Had a Word for Them* and *Tonight or Never*, with actress Gloria Swanson.

Greta Garbo, Claudette Colbert and Marlene Dietrich also became private
clients and were given a modern and truly Parisian look, on and off screen.

Chanel's introduction from Goldwyn
began a lasting relationship with
Hollywood and her American
clientele. Later, she would become
a favourie of Grace Kelly and
Elizabeth Taylor.

Grace
Kelly

Jackie Kennedy famously elevated the designer's tweed suit to iconic status during the 1960s.

Jackie Kennedy

"

a girl should
BE TWO THINGS:
classy
AND
fabulous

"

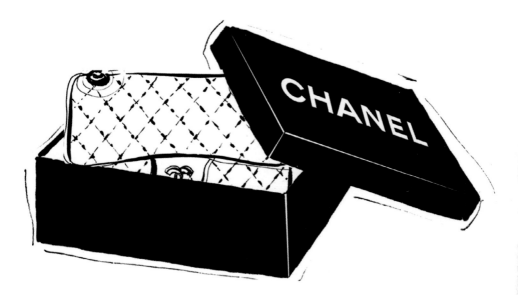

Chanel was one of the first designers to capture the potential of advertising. In 1937, the designer herself starred in the inaugural print campaign, photographed by revered fashion photographer François Kollar, featuring her in her apartment at the Hotel Ritz.

The Second World War severely
interrupted Chanel's operations and
she made the controversial decision
to close her haute couture salon in
1939 when France declared war
on Germany. *This is no time for
fashion,*' she announced.

CHANEL

At the time it was seen as an act of betrayal by her staff, which, by 1939 exceeded three thousand people. While other couturiers fled the country, Chanel saw the war out in Paris, remaining at the Hotel Ritz with her lover, an officer in the German army named Hans Günther von Dincklage.

When Paris was liberated in 1944, Chanel fled to Switzerland and did not return to Rue Cambon for almost a decade.

After fourteen years away from fashion, Chanel made
a comeback in 1954, returning to Paris to relaunch
the House of Chanel and take on Christian Dior's
overtly feminine New Look. As one fashion journalist
remarked, *'it was as though she had been out to lunch'*.
Though her return collection was not well
received, France's *Le Figaro* noted:
'You had a feeling you were back in 1925.'

Chanel persevered and soon gained her place as fashion's matriarch, continuing to pave the path for a new way of dressing.

THE NEWS

CHANEL
COLLECTION
DISAPPOINTED!

When Chanel revived her business in
1954, male designers such as Christian
Dior, Robert Piguet and Jacque Fath
dominated the fashion industry.
Chanel returned with her sensible
approach to style, rebelling against the
corseted aesthetics of male couturiers.

At age seventy, she had a renewed sense of passion and an intrinsic understanding of how modern women wanted to dress. Though France was slower to embrace her again, Chanel found immediate success in Britain and America. The couturier was back and this time she was here to stay.

" HOW MANY CARES *one loses* WHEN ONE DECIDES NOT *to be something* BUT *someone* "

Chanel never sketched her clothing like other designers, instead she cut straight into them. She would simply throw cloth onto a mannequin, cutting the shapeless mass of fabric until her desired silhouette emerged. Even into her old age, a pair of silver-plated scissors permanently dangled from Chanel's neck so she could make alterations as she made her way around the cutting-room floor.

N°5
CHANEL
PARIS
PARFUM

CHAN
31, RUE CAN

COCO CHANEL'S PARIS
CHANEL

Chanel might take a suit apart twenty times over to get the perfect fit. As *Harper's Bazaar* editor Diana Vreeland recalled, '*Coco was a nut on armholes. She never, ever got an armhole quite, quite perfect, the way she wanted it. She was always snipping and taking out sleeves, driving the tailors crazy.*'

Chanel would spend hours meticulously pinning, snipping and ripping. Only once the garment was perfected in *toile* would she create it in jersey, tweed, satin or lace.

Tired of carrying her handbag in her arms, Chanel designed a versatile and practical purse with straps during the 1920s, which would become her famous 2.55 bag.

Chanel revised and updated the design in 1955, releasing the iconic quilted purse that is so coveted today.

The design features remain: from the quilted leather in diamond proportions to the enclosing flap and her signature 'Mademoiselle Lock'.

Later, in 2005, the House of Chanel commemorated the fiftieth anniversary of the design by releasing an exact copy of the original 2.55.

The Classic Chanel two toned flat...

In 1957, Chanel turned her eye to footwear when she
released her classic two-tone shoe. The now-iconic shoe
used the contrast between beige and black to flatter the foot.
Raymond Massaro, the house shoemaker at the time, explained,
'The black, slightly square toe shortened the foot'.

Massaro would later work with couturiers such as
Thierry Mugler, Christian Lacroix and John Galliano,
but it was his work with Chanel that established
his credentials.

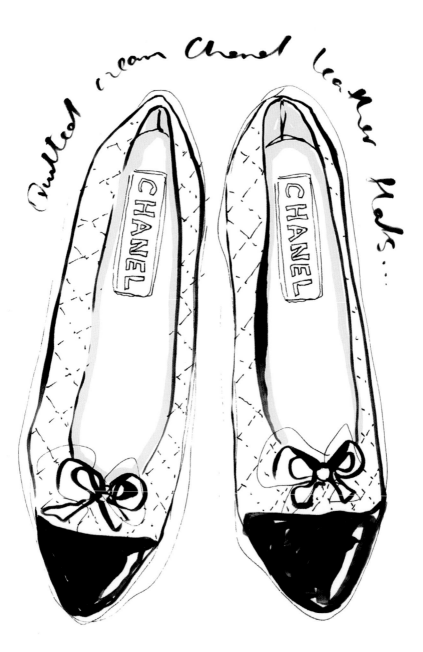

Quilted cream Chanel leather flats...

The Classic Chanel Two-tone Pumps

Chanel's own reasons for the design were simpler: the little heel made it easy to walk in, free to gallivant around, without visibly dirtying her shoes.

The two-tone slipper and its high-heeled adaptations remain a bestseller and an iconic symbol of the brand to this day.

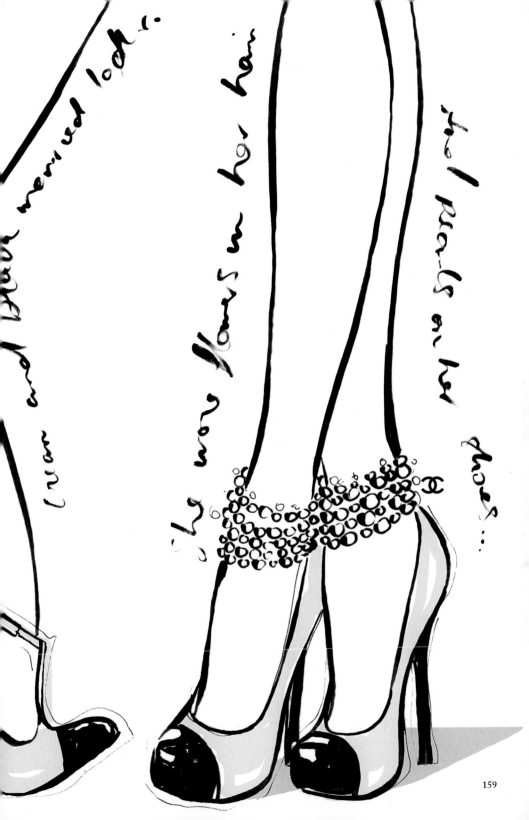

cream and black mermaid look...

She wore flowers in her hair

And pearls on her shoes...

159

"
a woman
WITH
good shoes
IS
never ugly
"

Though the House of Chanel has featured many cover girls, for Chanel N°5, the fragrance's most famous face would have to be Marilyn Monroe.

Marilyn Monroe

The actress, famous for wearing just a few drops of Chanel N°5 to bed, became an ambassador for the perfume when she was photographed in bed with a bottle placed on her nightstand.

N°5
CHANEL
PARIS

PARFUM

Suitably famous in the world of fashion, in 1969 Chanel's life was immortalised in a Broadway show, *Coco*. Written by Alan Jay Lerner with music by André Previn, the production starred Katharine Hepburn as Coco in the actress' first and only musical appearance.

Coco told the story of the couturier's early life to her comeback after years in retirement. Opening in New York at the Mark Hellinger Theatre to critical acclaim, Hepburn's performance was nominated for Best Actress at the 1970 Tony Awards.

the Legend

Though Coco Chanel passed away in 1971, her name lives on. Under the direction of Philippe Guibourgé, the house continued to produce haute couture, launching its first ready-to-wear collection in 1978. Today, Chanel is a luxury empire creating men's and womenswear, perfume, cosmetics and jewellery. It is a global brand with stores all over the world; however, one can still pilgrimage to 31 Rue Cambon in Paris to witness where it all began.

Since taking the helm in 1983, Karl Lagerfeld has revolutionised the brand, keeping the House of Chanel at the forefront of the fashion industry. The creative director has countlessly dipped into the archives, reviving the classics that the couturier pioneered. The label's hallmarks – from the tweed jacket to the Little Black Dress – remain staples alongside iconic accessories – the string of pearls and the quilted handbag – that have become symbols of status in a new generation. Coco Chanel herself endures as an influential figure in fashion, endlessly referenced for her infallible style. Chanel has come to embody the essence of the modern woman, as she once said: *'Fashion fades, only style remains the same.'*

Coco Chanel passed away in her sleep on
10 January 1971, at her apartment in the
Hotel Ritz. The couturier was eighty-seven
years old. Chanel worked up until her very
last day to complete her latest haute couture
collection. The day she died, her maid found
only three complete outfits in the closet of
her apartment.

Despite her reputation of being tough,
Chanel gave generously.

Perhaps remembering her own
humble roots when supporting
charitable causes, Chanel helped
others in the same manner she
designed: with purpose
and gusto.

The designer's funeral was held at L'église de la Madeleine, a church not far from Rue Cambon. Chanel's coffin was draped with white blooms, gardenias, orchids, azaleas and camellias, which were arranged symbolically in the shape of scissors.

Artist Salvador Dalí and actress Jeanne Moreau paid their respects, as did fellow couturiers Pierre Balmain, Cristóbal Balenciaga, André Courrèges and Yves Saint Laurent.

A fortnight after Chanel's death, the ivory tweed suits and white evening dresses she was working on were paraded down the runway at Paris Fashion Week, and met with a standing ovation.

After Chanel's death, Gaston Berthelot, coming from the House of Dior, took the reins as designer only to resign two years later. Design duo and former Chanel assistants, Yvonne Dudel and Jean Cazaubon, replaced Berthelot and in 1978 Philippe Guibourgé oversaw the House of Chanel's first ready-to-wear collection. In 1980, Balenciaga's former assistant Ramon Esparza signed on to oversee haute couture.

As artistic director of the House of Chanel, Philippe Guibourgé produced the atelier's first ready-to-wear collection in 1978. Like Yves Saint Laurent, Guibourgé recognised a new generation of women and a demand for off-the-rack luxury clothing. According to Guibourgé, the appeal of this new line was investment, not fantasy. He reintroduced Chanel's favourite jersey fabric in a collection of smart, navy suits. Without the numerous fittings required of haute couture, ready-to-wear also provided a more economic production process.

fitted to perfection

Chanel
Couture

CHANEL

House of Chanel once again began to make fashion headlines when Karl Lagerfeld came on board in 1982. Lagerfeld was born in Hamburg, Germany, on what is believed to be 10 September 1933. At age fourteen, he moved to Paris, becoming an assistant to couturier Pierre Balmain.

CHANEL

CH

He presented his first Chanel collection in January
1983 – the Spring/Summer Haute Couture Collection.
Today he is Artistic Director. As well as working for
Chanel, Lagerfeld has also worked with Fendi and Chloé,
launching his own line, Karl Lagerfeld, in 1984.

CHANEL

Like Coco, Karl Lagerfeld
mined the past as inspiration
for his collections. Continually
referencing classic Chanel
motifs, Lagerfeld incorporates
signature details such as tweed,
quilt-stitched leather, gold
chains and the interlocking
'C' logo into witty
reinventions.

CHANEL   CHANEL

A postmodern designer, Lagerfeld hit his stride at Chanel in the 1980s, reinventing her designs for a new era. Deconstructing Coco's classic polish while preserving the essence of the Chanel brand, he is undoubtedly one of the most influential men in fashion today.

CHANEL

Satisfying purists as well as inspiring bolder styles for more fashion-forward clients, the Chanel classics – the tweed jacket, the 2.55 bag and the strings of pearls – continue to be a mainstay for the brand.

Ever controversial and a genius of *pastiche*, Lagerfeld has successfully given Chanel designs countless makeovers.

His ability to reinvent the house and keep it relevant in the current market is a feat that has made him an iconic designer in his own right.

As Lagerfeld has said, *'Some things never go out of fashion in the world of fashion: jeans, the white shirt, and the Chanel jacket.'*

"

adornment,

WHAT A SCIENCE!

beauty,

WHAT A WEAPON!

modesty,

WHAT ELEGANCE!

"

Like Coco, Karl Lagerfeld values the elegance
and comfort of sportswear.

He has countlessly reinvented Chanel jersey
and embraced new markets with his signature
brand of 'sports luxe'.

Lagerfeld's adaptation of the interlocking
'C' logo has been another enduring gesture
by the designer, reflecting a similar marketing
intuition to Coco before him. While Chanel
borrowed from menswear, Lagerfeld also derived
his ideas from contemporary subcultures.

LADIES
FIRST
CHANEL

During the 1990s, he referenced everything from B-Boy styles to fetish fashions, creating PVC jeans, lace-up corsets – even dog collars – under the Chanel brand.

Karl Lagerfeld's signature of sampling the classic elements of the House of Chanel has given new life to Coco's legacy.

Karl's image is instantly recognisable: white ponytail, starched white shirt, tailored Hedi Slimane suit, biker gloves, topped off with his signature shades. Coco and Lagerfeld never met, but if they had? *'She would have hated me'*, Lagerfeld has said.

Despite this, the designer
continues to be inspired by
Chanel and her presence
remains in every collection,
*'I see her as the spirit
of the modern woman,'*
says Lagerfeld.

Karl Lagerfeld has continued
to build on the success of the
Chanel global empire, one that
regularly graces the pages
of style magazines and the
red carpet.

31

CHANEL

From the haute couture mini dress that Cameron Diaz showed off at the Golden Globes in 2003, to the frothy pink confection worn by Sarah Jessica Parker to the Academy Awards that same year, or the tiered gown Vanessa Paradis wore in 2004, the House of Chanel adorns many stars of today.

In 2015 Julianne Moore dazzled in a beaded strapless gown as she accepted her Academy Award for Best Actress. Lagerfeld stands beside many of the Chanel ambassadors, as a celebrity in his own right.

Since Lagerfeld took the helm, Chanel can always be counted on for its extravagant catwalk shows. Each season at Paris Fashion Week, fashion's elite gather in anticipation of what elaborate spectacle the designer has in store at the Grand Palais where the Chanel show is held.

CHANEL

In 2013, Lagerfeld transformed his runway into a supermarket sweep, allowing editors and models to shoplift from the aisles at the end of the show. In 2014, he staged a mock feminist march on a set he created of the streets of Paris.

In 2015, Lagerfeld imagined the catwalk as the fictional Brasserie Gabrielle, complete with waiters who served the models as they dined from the tables. As Michael Roberts, style director of *Vanity Fair* has said, *'His major strength is to be about his business in the present and never have a moment for other people to think that he's passé.'*

"

to achieve
GREAT THINGS,
we must
FIRST
dream

"

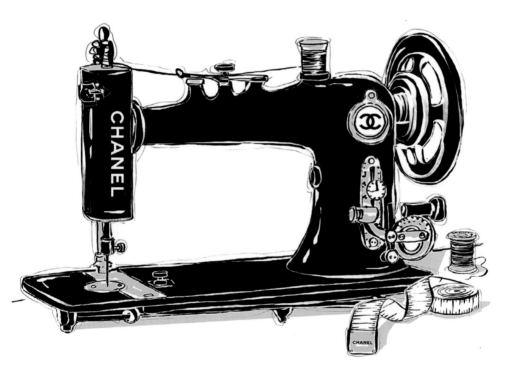

PARIS FASHION WEEK

CHANEL

In an industry seemingly obsessed
with trends, the House of Chanel remains
classic. Coco Chanel's modern approach
to fashion was revolutionary for her time,
emphasising comfort whilst looking chic.
From the Little Black Dress to the Chanel tweed
suit, the House of Chanel cultivates an elegant,
everlasting quality.

Karl Lagerfeld has continued Coco Chanel's legacy, reinventing the classics with a healthy dose of wit. His inimitable influence lies in the ability to adapt tradition to contemporary times: recreating Chanel classics to transforming the interlocking 'C' logo.

Patisserie

Most of all, Lagerfeld has continued Chanel's greatest trait of remaining original. As Coco once said herself, *'The most courageous act is still to think for yourself'*.

> "
> ## there are
> A LOT OF DUCHESSES,
> ## but there can
> ONLY BE ONE
> ## Coco Chanel
> "

Acknowledgements

To Paul McNally and Lucy Heaver for giving me the opportunity to illustrate Coco's life with passion and creativity.

To Meelee Soorkia for being the most wonderful editor and making sense of the hundreds and hundreds of Coco moments to create this book. We've pieced together so many details in Coco's story, I do feel you could have another life as a Tetris Master!

To Jo Barry, thank you for all the incredible research you did for this book. I thought I knew all there was to know about Mademoiselle Chanel but time after time you found more intricate details of her life. To Laura Gardner, thank you for turning the disparate parts of Coco's life into a story. To Murray Batten for your incredibly elegant design that does Coco justice. To Mark Campbell for your amazing design brain that makes my wildest ideas possible.

To Martina Granolic, thank you for casting your well-tuned eye over every single page of this book and being my reference point to all that is chic and 'Coco-worthy' to be included.

To Justine Clay for encouraging and supporting my work from the very beginning.

To my husband Craig, thank you for listening to me talk about Coco Chanel for 12 months straight and for sitting with me in 31 Rue Cambon for two hours while I 'Chaneled' Coco!

To my two children, Gwyn and Will. Even though you had no idea who Coco was in the begining, you still loved hearing her story. Both my children now prefer to wear their scissors on their necklaces just as Coco did!

About the author

Megan Hess was destined to draw. An initial career in graphic design evolved into art direction for some of the world's leading design agencies. In 2008 Hess illustrated the *New York Times* bestselling book *Sex and The City* by Candace Bushnell. She has since illustrated portraits for *Vanity Fair* and *Time*, created iconic illustrations for Cartier in Paris and illustrated the windows of Bergdorf Goodman in New York.

Hess's signature style can also be found on her bespoke Limited Edition Prints and homewares sold around the globe. Her renowned clients include Chanel, Dior, Tiffany & Co., Yves Saint Laurent, Vogue, Harpers Bazaar, Cartier, Balmain, Montblanc and The Ritz Hotel Paris.

When she's not in her studio working, you'll find her planning her next trip to 31 Rue Cambon in Paris to capture a little more of the magic that Mademoiselle Chanel first created.

Visit Megan at meganhess.com

Published in 2015 by Hardie Grant Books, an imprint of Hardie Grant Publishing

Hardie Grant Books (Melbourne)
Building 1, 658 Church Street
Richmond, Victoria 3121
hardiegrantbooks.com.au

Hardie Grant Books (London)
5th & 6th Floors
52-54 Southwark Street
London SE1 1UN
hardiegrantbooks.co.uk

All rights reserved. No part of this publication may be reproduced, stored in a
retrieval system or transmitted in any form by any means, electronic, mechanical,
photocopying, recording or otherwise, without the prior written permission of the
publishers and copyright holders.

The moral rights of the author have been asserted.

Copyright text and illustrations © Megan Hess 2015
Copyright design © Hardie Grant Publishing 2015

A Cataloguing-in-Publication entry is available from the catalogue of the National
Library of Australia at www.nla.gov.au

Coco Chanel: The Illustrated World of a Fashion Icon
ISBN 978 1 74379 066 3

Publishing Director: Paul McNally
Publisher: Lucy Heaver
Senior Editor: Meelee Soorkia
Editor: Laura Gardner
Design Manager: Mark Campbell
Designer: Murray Batten
Author photo: Martina Granolic
Production Manager: Todd Rechner

Colour reproduction by Splitting Image Colour Studio
Printed in China by 1010 Printing International Limited